Mason Jar Meals

38 Little-Known, Easy, Healthy & Delicious Mason Jar Recipes for Busy, On-the-Go People

Ella Marie

© 2015 Sender Publishing

© Copyright 2015 by Sender Publishing - All rights reserved.

This document is geared towards providing exact and reliable information in regards to the topic and issue covered. The publication is sold with the idea that the publisher is not required to render accounting, officially permitted, or otherwise, qualified services. If advice is necessary, legal or professional, a practiced individual in the profession should be ordered.

From a Declaration of Principles which was accepted and approved equally by a Committee of the American Bar Association and a Committee of Publishers and Associations.

In no way is it legal to reproduce, duplicate, or transmit any part of this document in either electronic means or in printed format. Recording of this publication is strictly prohibited and any storage of this document is not allowed unless with written permission from the publisher. All rights reserved.

The information provided herein is stated to be truthful and consistent, in that any liability, in terms of inattention or otherwise, by any usage or abuse of any policies, processes, or directions contained within is the solitary and utter responsibility of the recipient reader. Under no circumstances will any legal responsibility or blame be held against the publisher for any reparation, damages, or monetary loss due to the information herein, either directly or indirectly.

Respective authors own all copyrights not held by the publisher.

The information herein is offered for informational purposes solely, and is universal as so. The presentation of the information is without contract or any type of guarantee assurance.

The ideas, concepts and/or opinions delivered in this book are to be used for educational purposes only. This book is provided with the understanding that authors and publisher are not rendering medical advice of any kind, nor is this book intended to replace medical advice, nor to diagnose, prescribe or treat any disease, condition, illness or injury.

It is imperative that before beginning any diet or exercise program, including any aspect of this book, you receive full medical clearance from a licensed doctor and/or physician. Author and publisher claim no responsibility to any person or entity for any liability, loss, or damage caused or alleged to be caused directly or indirectly as a result of the use, application or interpretation of the material in this book.

The trademarks that are used are without any consent, and the publication of the trademark is without permission or backing by the trademark owner. All trademarks and brands within this book are for clarifying purposes only and are owned by the owners themselves, not affiliated with this document.

For more books by this author, please visit:

www.wellnessbooks.net

Table of Contents

Introduction 1

Chapter 1: Why Are Mason Jar Meals So Popular? 3

Chapter 2: Getting Started 7

Chapter 3: Tips For Creating Your Mason Jar Meals Successfully .. 10

Chapter 4: Breakfast Recipes 14

Chapter 5: Lunch Recipes 27

Chapter 6: Salad Recipes 31

Chapter 7: Dinner Recipes 39

Chapter 8: Dessert Recipes 46

Conclusion 59

Introduction

Are you looking for new meal ideas? Do you often reach for processed or fast food because you don't have something already prepared? Though no one is going to wave a magic wand and make that food appear, you shouldn't give up!

Many of us are in the same boat—we need meals *fast*. With some smart organization and prepping, however, you can make amazing meals that aren't time consuming. Mason jar meals and desserts are becoming much more common. This method can be an exciting way to change your mindset about creating meals and taking your lunch to work.

Mason jar meals look and taste great, and they may be exactly what you've been looking for. Many people have pre-existing ideas about mason jar meals—namely, that they don't allow for much variety. This belief prevents them from pursuing jarred meals as an option.

But this couldn't be further from the truth! There are plenty of great recipes you can try using mason jars. What's fun is that you can vary them in any way to suit your needs and preferences. For instance, you can add ingredients to the salad recipes or switch fruits in the dessert recipes, and that's just the beginning.

No one wants to eat the same thing day after day, but in today's world, convenience often trumps all other considerations. By making mason jar meals, it's possible to achieve that variety while simultaneously using foods that are good for you. As you discover great recipes, you will also start to feel comfortable creating some of your own.

Creating mason jar meals that your family will love is only going to encourage you to continue. You can plan your meals in advance and get all of the ingredients in one, organized trip to the store. You can then feel better about what you eat and what you feed your family.

You'll also stop feeling guilty about the bad food choices you made in the past when you were in a hurry. Mason jars are grab-and-go, but also allow you to see the ingredients inside, so you know you're making healthy choices. Some jarred recipes are served as-is, while others only need to be shaken up before you eat them.

Eating out, while easy and convenient, can add a huge expense to the monthly budget. By planning your meals and getting some mason jars, you are going to slash what you spend on food. And at the same time, you'll be eating healthier, feel more satisfied, and *won't* spend tons of time in the kitchen

By the time you are finished reading this book, you will have plenty of answers and the encouragement to begin. You will understand how to get started, learn the best practices, and explore amazing recipes.

You are also going to realize that you have the power to make it happen! You don't have to love spending time in the kitchen to make mason jar meals. You don't have to own an endless supply of ingredients, either. In fact, several of the recipes you will read about include only a few ingredients.

If you want to seize an opportunity to eat better and in an all-around positive way, it is right in front of you. This book is going to give you the inspiration and confidence to start making mason jar meals. Be ready for tons of complements from your family, friends, and co-workers once you do!

Chapter 1
Why Are Mason Jar Meals So Popular?

When there is something new happening, people take notice. They often want to learn first-hand what all of the fuss is about. Many of these new things, however, just become passing trends. They seem to lose the interest of the consumers just as quickly as they began.

This doesn't seem to be the case with mason jar meals. In fact, they are really picking up in popularity. They work well for all age groups, including families, college students, baby boomers, retirees, and those in the business force. The truth is that everyone needs to eat.

With that in mind, mason jar meals make a great deal of sense. They allow for more control over what you are eating. When your life is fast-paced and busy, poor eating habits are very easy to develop. Cutting out processed foods and fast foods can help you slash many of these bad habits.

You will also find that most of the mason jar meals contain ingredients that are good for you. They have plenty of protein, such as chicken and lean meats. They also include plenty of antioxidants and make you feel more energetic due to the fresh fruits and vegetables they contain.

There are some great desserts too, but as the portions are smaller, you don't have to feel guilty for consuming them now and then. Plus, if you are cutting out calories in other ways, your diet will allow for those occasional sweet treats which won't result in weight gain or health problems.

Making food convenient as well as visually appealing is important. We don't want to eat food that is boring, bland, or colorless day after day. Mason jars offer a simple but elegant way to serve a variety of dishes. They are also easy to wash and aren't expensive to purchase.

These meals are becoming increasingly popular as people learn about and share them. All it will take is eating one—at a luncheon, or at a friend's house—to get you hooked! You might have also seen mason jar meals on Pinterest and would like to try them.

Let's face it—we all get tired of the same old routine when it comes to eating and making meals. We often do it robotically, but now is the time to change that. You'll be looking forward to lunch again when you see your colorful mason jar instead of a brown paper sack containing a dull sandwich.

The possibilities are endless when it comes to mason jars: you can use them for salads and other cold foods; you can put them in the oven and bake directly inside them; you can even microwave them if you are in a hurry. The fact that glass is 100% recyclable only adds to the positives. Knowing that you are doing your part to reduce waste in the environment is always a good feeling.

Mason jars store well, too. You won't need to use lots of pots and pans for cooking and tupperware containers for storing. Glass mason jars offer an all-in-one solution.

College dorms with kitchens are often stocked with mason jars. This type of cooking has become very popular among college students, because it's easy and hassle-free. If busy—but often lazy—teenagers can do it, so can you.

Eating healthier and being aware of what you're putting into your body is a driving force behind the explosion of mason jar meals. People are finally understanding that processed fast foods aren't good for the mind or the body.

Making healthy choices doesn't mean you must eat food that tastes bad or go hungry. Instead, you can eat foods that offer you nutrition and look appealing to you. Of course, there *are* mason jar meals and desserts that aren't the healthiest, so take care to eat those in moderation!

With mason jars, you can see exactly how much food you are eating. Portion control is a huge problem in our society today. Think about when you serve plates in your kitchen. Most of us don't measure the amount of food that we pile on a plate.

Think, too, about when you go to eat out or drive up to a window. Most fast food restaurants try to entice you by inexpensively upsizing your sides, such as French fries or a soft drink. This results in consuming far more calories than is necessary or healthy.

Most sit down restaurants offer portions that are even larger than what we would serve ourselves at home. Yet, since we are paying for the meal and we are enjoying the atmosphere, we tend to eat more than we normally would. If you show up starving, you may even get an appetizer, too.

Mason jar meals, though, help you simply and successfully identify how much food you are consuming. Getting your portion sizes under control is one of the key ways to reduce calorie intake and, consequently, lose weight.

It is also a part of a healthy lifestyle. Simply being conscious about serving sizes is an eye-opening experience and a step in the right direction towards better, overall health.

While you may have your own reasons for trying out mason jar meals, here are the most common reasons others have suggested:

- Mason jars are dishwasher safe.
- They can be reused.
- They are not harmful to the environment.
- Foods don't stain glass jars.
- Layered and colorful mason jars are visually appealing.
- They are easy to stack, pack, transport, and shake.
- They are inexpensive to buy.

- Mason jars can be stored in the refrigerator, frozen, placed in the microwave, or put into the oven.
- They are convenient.
- Mason jar meals are easy to re-heat.
- They are easy to store.

As you try out these recipes and create your mason jar meals, feel free to add some of your own reasons to this list!

Chapter 2
Getting Started

Perhaps you love the idea of mason jar meals, but are feeling skeptical. The last thing you want is a troublesome endeavor in the kitchen. You don't have to spend lots of time or lots of money, however, to give these meals a try.

You may find you already have several of the items you need around the house. If not, it isn't going to cost much money at all to get them. Here is what you need to get started:

- A few mason jars
- Some recipes to try
- A shopping list
- Time to plan

A Few Mason Jars

Buying mason jars of various sizes is highly recommended. You will find as you look for recipes that the sizes of the required jars will vary. While 4-ounce and 8-ounce jars are the most common sizes, they aren't the only ones to consider. And if the jars you have aren't the right size, you can reduce or increase the ingredients proportionally, but make sure your calculations are correct.

Buy mason jars with lids so you can easily store your leftovers. This is also important for meals such as salads. You need a good fitting lid so you can shake up all the ingredients without making a mess.

You can buy cases of mason jars from many retailers that you already visit. You can also buy them in bulk, if you want to acquire a lot of them. Cases don't cost very much, and you will find that buying them as a set is far less expensive per unit than buying the jars individually. There are even some websites where you can buy mason jars with lids and have them shipped directly to your home.

Look for those that offer free or low-cost shipping. Mason jars can be heavy so you don't want to pay a fortune for the shipping. Always consider the total cost of the product plus shipping fees.

Some Recipes to Try

Find a few recipes that you would initially like to try. When you are successful with them, you will be encouraged to continue and expand your repertoire. If you don't have much spare time, you can look for recipes with a low prep time and just a few ingredients.

If you are interested in losing weight or eating better, look for recipes that include ingredients that are highly nutritional. There are even mason jar desserts that have plenty of fruit and yogurt in them. They will satisfy your sweet-tooth without being loaded with sugar and calories.

You can find all the recipes you need online. There are websites that not only show you the ingredients, but also provide step-by-step photos of the preparation process. Of course, this book will provide you with quite a few recipes to try. Once you are done exploring those, it will be easy to seek out some of your own.

Pinterest has become a very popular place for mason jar recipes. If you are looking for a particular recipe, it's the best website to start searching for it. You can search by ingredients, health benefits, or even prep time.

A Shopping List

Now that you have your recipes, get your shopping list ready. Knowing what you need before you arrive at the grocery store is very important. It will make the shopping process faster, more efficient, and thorough: you won't have to return later for any ingredients you forgot, and you'll be less likely to be distracted by unhealthy, calorie-laden "convenience" foods. Try to find items that are in season, as well. This can help you to cut costs and increase nutritional values.

For example, you can substitute fruits and vegetables within recipes for whatever is in stock, fresh, and low-priced. Many ingredients can also be substituted with foods that are more affordable or more to your tastes.

Time to Plan

You have to allot time for cooking meals anyway, so why not use some of that time to create mason jar ones? For example, if breakfast is often a hassle in your home, you can do the prep the night before. Many of these great recipe options allow you to make the food ahead of time, and refrigerate it until use.

Even the recipes that need to be baked can be prepped in advance. Just store them in the fridge until you're nearly ready to eat. Then preheat the oven, and pop them in, while you continue with your other activities.

The mason jars will be ready when you are. This is especially true and helpful for hot breakfasts. It's a simple plan that takes minimal time, so you can start the day off with great-tasting, nutritious food.

Chapter 3
Tips For Creating Your Mason Jar Meals Successfully

Before you dive right into creating mason jar meals, you should be aware of these helpful tips. They will reduce the time involved in prep and clean-up. They will also help you achieve the best quality results.

Greasing

Many foods can stick to the sides of your mason jars if you aren't careful. Greasing may be recommended by the recipe and if so, it's a step you shouldn't skip. It can be difficult to get your hands to the bottom of the mason jar to scrub it clean.

Using spray cooking spray is the best option for greasing your mason jars. It is very simple to use, even if you have larger hands, because you can simply aim the spray into the mouth of the jar. This also means that you will avoid the frustration of sticking food when cleaning up.

Cleaning

Make sure you clean the mason jars very well. You may need to get a bottle brush or other tool if you can't reach the bottom of the jars. You can also place them into your dishwasher which will clean and sanitize them.

It is very important to make sure the mason jars are completely clean. Otherwise, germs will linger and bacteria can grow.

Another common problem is not thoroughly rinsing if you wash them by hand. The lingering soap can ruin the taste of your next recipe, so rinse them well. Imagine taking the time to make something delicious and then tasting soap instead—that's an error you'd be happier avoiding altogether.

Inspecting

Mason jars are very durable, but you do have to be careful with them. The glass can break or chip. Always inspect the mason jars after you wash them and before you put them away. Check the handles so you don't cut yourself when picking one up. Check around the lid area, too, as that is a common place for chipping to occur.

If you notice any issues with a mason jar, don't continue to use it. Instead, it should be recycled with your other glass items.

To help reduce problems with mason jars, buy ones of good quality. They aren't going to cost much more, but the quality difference can be significant. Take good care of the mason jars, too. Handle them gently, and don't bang them together.

Handling

Mason jars will be extremely hot when you take them out of the oven. Make sure you handle them with care to avoid serious burns. Don't leave them to cool where children or pets can access them.

Even if the outside of the mason jar is only warm, the food contents inside of it can still be very hot. Don't be in a rush to put that food onto a utensil and into your mouth! Always check it first so you don't burn your tongue.

Baking

It is a good idea to place a baking pan or cookie sheet underneath the mason jars before you bake in them. This will make it much easier to remove the hot jars from the oven. When you slide them into the oven, however, do so gently so they don't tip over. This can result in a huge mess to clean up.

Some recipes will tell you to add a few inches of water to the bottom of the cooking pan. This is to ensure that the ingredients on the bottom of the mason jars don't burn. Pay attention to such tips, as they can make a huge difference in your resulting meal.

Following Directions

Make sure you take the time to follow the directions with mason jar foods. Use the right size of jar for the item you are making. You can reduce or increase the amount of jars the food is for but make sure you do the math right so you have the right amount of ingredients.

If you don't follow the directions your mason jar meals may be a flop. You may end up creating a mess too by over filling the jars. Some of the food items will expand during baking so read what the recipe says and you can avoid such concerns.

If you are easily intimidated when it comes to trying something new, start out slow. Use recipes that have only 5 or fewer ingredients. Make sure you like what the ingredients include. The last thing you want is to put forth the time and effort and then toss out what you have just made.

Storing

The recipe should also tell you how long you can store the mason jar meals after making them. Typically it will be from 3 to 5 days, but this depends on the types of ingredients. Make sure the mason jar foods are secured with lids that fit correctly, and consume the food in a timely manner to prevent food-related illnesses.

If you often make mason jar meals, it's a great idea to label them with both the contents and the use-by date. Use labels that stick well but wash off easily in water. You can also label with a dry-erase marker, as long as you don't smudge the information with your fingers.

Having Fun!

Creating mason jar meals should be fun, not stressful, work! Have a good time experimenting. You may decide that you want to create some of your own recipes based off of others you have found. Or perhaps you would like to substitute certain ingredients to make a recipe more to your own liking.

You don't have to make mason jar meals on your own either. You can make it a family activity. Set aside an hour or two on the weekend when you can all participate.

You can try new recipes, clean up together, and talk as you prepare the meals. This is going to make the entire process more fun, as well as socially and healthily beneficial for the entire family.

Chapter 4
Breakfast Recipes

Breakfast is the most important meal of the day, yet so many people skip it due to the morning rush. Creating these amazing mason jar breakfast recipes will ensure you get the day off to a great start. Some of them you can even make the night before, which helps to eliminate the hectic morning rush that many households experience!

Since the food is in a mason jar, you can also take your meal to-go. Perhaps you have a long commute to the office in the morning. You can enjoy your food on the drive. You can even take it into the office for consuming at your desk while you go through your emails and organize your daily tasks.

BAKED EGGS

6 mason jars, 4 ounces each

2 teaspoons organic olive oil
1 organic onion, sliced
1 cup organic asparagus, chopped
10 free-range eggs, beaten
1 cup grass-fed cheese, grated

Preheat oven to 375°F. Heat the oil in a skillet and add the onions. Sauté them for a couple of minutes. Add the asparagus and cook for about 5 minutes—until it is tender but still crisp. Add salt and pepper to taste.

Generously grease the mason jars. Use tongs to add the vegetable mixture. Beat the eggs well and add them to the mason jars. Distribute the cheese on top. Use a spoon to stir the jars well so the cheese mixes in with the eggs and vegetables.

Bake for 20 to 25 minutes. The tops should be golden brown. Remove from the oven and allow to cool. You can add the lids and store once the jars are completely cool. It's also possible to prepare enough jars for a whole week of breakfasts. Now getting breakfast ready in a hurry isn't a problem.

Ella Marie

PEACHES & CREAM FRENCH TOAST

8 mason jars, 4 ounces each

1 cup organic flour
1 tablespoon baking powder
3-ounce box instant vanilla pudding mix
3 tablespoons grass-fed butter
1 free-range egg
½ cup half-and-half
16-ounce can peach halves
8-ounce package of organic cream cheese, softened
½ cup coconut sugar
8 pieces of organic bread

Preheat oven to 350°F. Mix all of the ingredients except the peaches and bread in a large bowl for 2 minutes on medium speed. Place a piece of bread at the bottom of each mason jar. Drain the peaches and add a few slices to each jar. Pour the batter over the bread and peaches.

Bake for 30 minutes. The top should be bubbling. Eat warm. To prevent the ingredients from sticking to the mason jars, generously grease them prior to use.

BANANA KIWI BREAKFAST YOGURT

6 mason jars, 4 ounces each

Granola:
1 cup organic gluten-free oats
½ cup coconut, shredded
2 tablespoons organic brown sugar
A pinch of cinnamon
3 tablespoons coconut oil
2 tablespoons raw honey

Yogurt:
2 cups organic vanilla yogurt
2 cups organic strawberry yogurt
1 organic banana, chopped
2 organic kiwis, chopped

Mix all of the ingredients together to make the granola mixture. In a separate bowl, mix the yogurt and the fruit. Layer the granola and yogurt in the mason jars. Refrigerate for a couple of hours before eating.

BANANA NUT BREAD

8 mason jars, pint-sized

2/3 cup shortening
2 ½ cups coconut sugar
4 free-range eggs
2 cups organic bananas, mashed
1 cup water
3 ½ cups organic all-purpose flour
½ teaspoon baking powder
2 teaspoons baking soda
1 teaspoon himalayan salt
1 teaspoon cinnamon
1 teaspoon cloves, ground
1 cup pecans, chopped

Preheat oven to 325°F. Grease the sides and bottoms of the mason jars. In a mixing bowl, cream the shortening and salt until it is fluffy. Add the bananas, eggs, and water. Mix well and put aside.

In another mixing bowl, sift together the flour, baking soda, baking powder, cloves, cinnamon, and salt. Add the liquid mixture to the dry mixture and stir well. Add the nuts last. Fill each jar ½ full as the mixture will rise as the banana bread bakes.

Bake for 45 minutes or until the banana bread is golden brown on the top. It should also be pulling away from the glass as it firms up. The jars can be sealed and kept in the refrigerator for about a week after making.

BREAKFAST CASSEROLE

6 mason jars, 4 ounces each

6 free-range eggs
½ cup organic milk
1 can crescent roll dough
1 roll sausage, cooked, crumbled, drained
1 cup grass-fed cheddar cheese, shredded

Place one crescent roll dough piece firmly to the bottom of each mason jar. Cook the sausage and drain all of the grease. You can also make this breakfast casserole with bacon instead of sausage if you prefer.

Mix the eggs and milk together. Pour evenly into the mason jars. Divide the cheese and add to the top of each jar. Bake at 350°F for 20 minutes.

BACON AND EGGS

6 mason jars, 4 ounces each

6 free-range eggs
1 cup grass-fed cheese, shredded
1 lb nitrate-free bacon, cooked, drained, crumbled

Mix the eggs and cheese in a bowl, then pour into the mason jars. Place each mason jar into the microwave for about 2 minutes. This will cause the egg mixture to puff up. However, it will deflate soon.

Mix in cheese and bacon. You can also add some fresh spinach to the mixture if you like.

COCO BANANA OATMEAL

This recipe is for one mason jar

¼ cup organic rolled oats, uncooked
1/3 cup almond milk
14 cup organic vanilla yogurt
2 tablespoons chia seeds
1 tablespoon cocoa
½ cup organic banana, chopped

Mix the oats, yogurt, almond milk, and chia seeds into the mason jar. Put the lid on tightly and shake well. Add the cocoa and stir well. Add the bananas. Add 1 tablespoon chopped walnuts and one tablespoon honey to this recipe if desired.

It is best to let this mixture refrigerate for several hours before consuming. Ideally, make it the night before and enjoy in the morning. Make sure you consume this product within 3 days of making it due to the dairy ingredients it includes.

MINIATURE CINNAMON ROLLS

4 mason jars, 4 ounces each

2 cups organic all-purpose flour, unbleached
2 tablespoons coconut sugar
¼ teaspoon baking powder
½ teaspoon himalayan salt
¼ cup grass-fed butter, cut into pieces
¾ cup organic buttermilk

Mix all of the dry ingredients in a large mixing bowl. Cut in the pieces of butter and mix in well. The dough should be crumbly. Add the buttermilk and mix. The dough should start to form. Add some flour to the countertop and knead for 2 minutes. Roll into a large rectangle about ¼" thick.

¼ cup grass-fed butter, softened
1 cup organic brown sugar
1 teaspoon cinnamon

Mix the ingredients well and spread over the rectangle dough. Roll the dough away from you. Cut in half, in half again, and then into thirds. You will have 12 even sized slices.

Grease the bottom of the mason jars and place them on a cookie sheet. Add 3 of the slices to each mason jar. Bake at 350°F for 18 minutes. The tops should be golden brown. Allow them to cool before eating. While they are cooling, you can make the icing.

2 cups organic powdered sugar
¼ cup organic heavy cream
1 tablespoon vanilla

Whisk the ingredients together in a bowl. Add more cream if needed to get the desired consistency. Spoon on top of the cinnamon rolls.

Ella Marie

CINNAMON PANCAKES

6 mason jars, 4 ounces each

6 cups organic flour, unbleached
1 tablespoon baking powder
3 tablespoons coconut sugar
2 tablespoons cinnamon
1 tablespoon himalayan salt

Mix all of the ingredients well in a mixing bowl. Use a wire whisk, not an electric mixer. Add an even amount of the batter to each of the 6 mason jars. Bake at 350°F for 10 minutes.

STRAWBERRY BANANA CHEWY OATS

** Ingredients are per mason jar**

½ cup organic rolled oats
½ cup organic Greek yogurt
2/3 cup organic milk
1 tablespoon chia seeds
1 organic banana, mashed
2 tablespoons organic strawberry jam

Mix all the ingredients together well. Place into the mason jar and put a lid on it tightly. Allow it to refrigerate overnight.

Ella Marie

BANANA & ALMOND SMOOTHIE

** Ingredients are per pint-size mason jar**

1 cup almond milk
1 tablespoon organic almond butter
1 organic banana
1 tablespoon flaxseed, ground

Blend all of the ingredients and then pour them into the mason jar. Refrigerate for a couple of hours before consuming. Can be made the night before for a delicious and nutritious smoothie to drink in the morning.

Chapter 5
Lunch Recipes

Getting a great tasting lunch while you are at work or just busy around the house is important. Otherwise, you may skip lunch or grab something that isn't very nutritious. Here are some great mason jar lunch recipes to try!

SUSHI IN A JAR

** Ingredients are for 1 mason jar**

½ cup organic short grain, brown rice, cooked
1 teaspoon coconut sugar
2 teaspoons soy sauce
1 Nori sheet, cut into ¼" pieces
½ cup mixture of organic cucumbers and carrots, shredded
¼ cup organic avocado, diced
1 tablespoon lime juice
1 tablespoon ginger, pickled
¼ cup wasabi paste

In a small saucepan, heat the sugar and soy sauce. Heat until the sugar is dissolved. Heat the brown rice and pour this mixture over the top of it while it is still warm.

Coat the avocado with the lime juice so it won't turn brown. Mix in the rest of the vegetables with the avocado. You are ready to start layering your ingredients. Place half of the Nori at the bottom and the half at the top.

MEDITERRANEAN QUINOA

6 or 8 mason jars, 4 ounces or larger each

1 cup organic red or white quinoa, rinsed
2 cups water or organic vegetable broth
½ cup vinaigrette
2 teaspoons whole grain mustard
3 tablespoons lemon juice, fresh squeezed
1 tablespoon white wine vinegar
2 cloves organic garlic, minced
¼ teaspoon crushed red pepper flakes
½ cup olive oil, extra virgin preferred
1 cucumber, diced
2 cups whole kernel corn
1 pint organic cherry tomatoes, halved
1 organic red onion, sliced
½ cup organic parsley, finely chopped

Boil the quinoa and water or broth over high heat. Reduce the heat to simmer once it is at a full boil. Allow it to simmer for about 15 minutes, until the quinoa is tender. Remove from heat and cover. Allow it to sit for 5 more minutes. Use a fork to fluff. The quinoa can be prepared the day before.

Mix all of the vegetables together. Then mix in the remaining ingredients, including the quinoa. Place the mixture generously into the mason jars. It can be stored for up to 3 days as long as it is refrigerated.

CORN DOGS

12 mason jars, at least ½ pint in size

3 cups yellow corn meal, self rising
6 free-range eggs
1 ½ cup organic milk
½ cup organic sour cream
¼ cup grape seed oil
¾ cup coconut sugar
6 organic hot dogs, cut in half

Preheat oven to 375°F. Mix all of the ingredients except the hot dogs. The mixture should be smooth. Generously grease the bottom and sides of each mason jar. Add the mixture evenly to each jar.

Stand a hot dog upright in the center of the batter in each mason jar. Bake for 20 minutes. The corn bread should be golden brown. Allow them to cool down completely. Use a knife to loosen the corn bread from the sides of the mason jars.

You can eat immediately or refrigerate until you are ready to eat. To reheat, remove the lid and microwave for 45 seconds to 1 minute. You can enjoy it alone or with mustard and ketchup. Chili and cheese can be added for additional flavors, too.

Ella Marie

LAYERED BURRITOS

4 large mason jars

1 cup organic quinoa, cooked
1 ½ cups organic black beans
4 cups organic lettuce, chopped
1 cup organic kale, chopped
1 cup sunflower spouts
2 cups organic salsa
1 cup organic Greek yogurt, plain

Cook quinoa and allow it to cool. Add ¼ cup to the bottom of each mason jar. Add the black beans, lettuce, kale, salsa, yogurt, and then sprouts in that order. Make sure you leave some room at the top. Shake well before eating. Make burritos out of the mixture or eat with tortillas on the side.

Chapter 6
Salad Recipes

A healthy salad is a great way to stay on track with your weight loss efforts or your healthy eating objectives. These mason jar salads will stop you from putting money into the vending machine or going to the local drive-thru to grab something for lunch.

One of the common questions people have when it comes to mason jar salads is how to coat the ingredients well. Most of the recipes tell you to put the dressing at the bottom of the jar. Just make sure to leave space at the top so you can shake it all around before you eat it. Don't pack the mason jar so full that it doesn't move when you shake it.

Another common concern is the lettuce will wilt. However, with many of these recipes, even after sitting in the jars for a few days, the lettuce doesn't have to be wilted. It can stay crisp and delicious. The secret to making sure that happens is to get mason jars with good-fitting lids. An air-tight seal will reduce the risk of such problems.

Ella Marie

TURKEY & CORNBREAD SALAD

6 mason jars, 3 or 4 ounces each

6 ounces buttermilk cornbread mix
12 ounces organic Parmesan-Peppercorn dressing
¼ cup organic buttermilk
½ cup organic mayonnaise
1 package organic Romaine lettuce, shredded
3 cups organic turkey, smoked and chopped
2 organic bell peppers, any color, chopped
2 organic tomatoes, chopped
1 organic onion, chopped
1 cup organic celery, diced
2 cups organic Swiss cheese, shredded
1 lb nitrate-free bacon, cooked, drained, crumbled
2 organic green onions, sliced

Follow the directions on the packaging to make the cornbread. Allow it to cool then crumble. Place a layer of the cornbread at the bottom of each mason jar.

Mix the buttermilk, mayonnaise, and dressing together well. Mix the remaining ingredients together. Generously place into the mason jars. Add the dressing to the top. Make sure there is enough room at the top of the jar for you to shake well before eating. For the best results allow this salad to refrigerate for at least 3 hours before eating.

TACO SALAD

4 mason jars, 12 ounces each

2 organic chicken breasts, grilled
1 cup organic black beans
1 cup organic corn
1 cup organic tomatoes, diced
1 cup organic romaine lettuce, chopped

For the dressing:
½ cup organic Greek yogurt
½ cup organic goat cheese, crumbled
¼ cup organic cilantro, fresh
1 organic lime, juiced
¼ teaspoon cumin
¼ teaspoon himalayan salt, optional
1 organic avocado
¼ cup water

Add all of the ingredients for the dressing and blend well. Puree until smooth and refrigerate for 30 minutes so it can thicken. Shred the grilled chicken. Place ¼ cup of the dressing at the bottom of each mason jar.

Add the following in this order: corn, black beans, tomatoes, chicken, and lettuce. For best results allow it to refrigerate a few hours before consuming. Shake well and pour over corn chips when ready to eat.

Ella Marie

BEET & CARROT SALAD

** recipe is per pint-sized mason jar**

½ cup carrots, julienned
¼ cup red wine vinaigrette
½ cup organic beets, quartered
2 ounces goat cheese, crumbled
2 cups organic spinach leaves

Pour the vinaigrette into the bottom of the mason jar. Add the other ingredients and put the lid on tightly. Make sure there is enough room to shake well before eating.

CAPRESE SALAD

2 mason jars, pint-sized

2 organic tomatoes, red or green, sliced
½ cup mozzarella cheese, shredded
¼ cup balsamic vinaigrette
8 organic basil leaves, fresh

Place the vinaigrette at the bottom of the mason jars. Add the other ingredients. Make sure you have enough room to shake it all up before you eat it. This will ensure all of the ingredients are well-coated with the dressing.

Ella Marie

ASIAN NOODLE SALAD

4 mason jars, 4 ounces each

4 ounces Soba noodles
1 bell pepper, sliced
1 cup edamame, shelled, cooked
2 organic carrots, peeled and shredded
4 organic green onions, sliced
1 cup crunchy noodles

For the dressing:
2 tablespoons organic peanut butter
4 teaspoons rice vinegar
4 tablespoons soy sauce
¼ cup cold-pressed organic olive oil, extra virgin
4 teaspoons Sambal Oelek
1 tablespoon sesame seeds

Boil a pot of water and add the noodles. Cook until they are tender. Rinse with cold water and drain well. Allow the noodles to completely cool.

In a mixing bowl add the ingredients for the dressing. Mix very well. Add the dressing to the bottom of the four mason jars. Add the Soba noodles. Layer the remaining ingredients any way you desire, with the crunchy noodles on top. Make sure you leave enough room in the jar to shake well before eating.

WHEAT BERRY APPLE SALAD

4 mason jars, any size

3 cups wheat berries, cooked
1 cup organic apples, chopped
½ cup organic cranberries, dried
1 scallion, minced
1 tablespoon lemon juice
1 tablespoon balsamic vinegar
1 tablespoon cold-pressed organic extra virgin olive oil
2 tablespoons organic parsley, chopped

Whisk the balsamic vinegar, olive oil, and lemon juice well. In another bowl add the remaining ingredients and mix well. Pour the liquid mix over the salad mix. Use your hands to toss it well. Distribute the salad mixture evenly into the mason jars. Refrigerate for a few hours before eating.

Ella Marie

WILD RICE SALAD

4 mason jars, 4 ounces each

1 cup organic wild rice
½ cup organic cranberries, dried
½ cup pecans, chopped
½ cup cashews, unsalted, chopped
¼ cup organic celery, chopped
¼ cup organic onion, chopped

Dressing:
⅛ cup red wine vinegar
1 tablespoon lemon juice
1 organic garlic clove, minced
1 teaspoon mustard
1 teaspoon coconut sugar
1/3 cup cold-pressed organic extra virgin olive oil

In a saucepan boil, 4 cups of water and 1 tablespoon salt. Once it comes to a full boil, add the rice. Reduce to medium heat and cover. Simmer for about 45 minutes, the rice should be tender. Stir occasionally. Allow the rice to completely cool. Drain so there is no water left.

In a blender, mix the lemon juice, garlic, sugar, mustard, and vinegar. Pour in the olive oil last and blend it in well. Allow this to sit while you add the rest of the ingredients to the rice. Next, pour this dressing over the rice mixture. Distribute into jars.

Chapter 7
Dinner Recipes

After a busy day of work, the last thing you want to do is plan and cook dinner. Don't be tempted to order pizza or to grab burgers on your way home from a drive-thru window. Instead, consider these perfect mason jar dinner options!

CHICKEN CORDON BLEU

6 mason jars, 6 ounces each

6 chicken breasts
1 tablespoon salt
½ teaspoon black pepper
6 slices ham
6 slices Swiss cheese
½ cup butter, melted, unsalted
2 cups bread crumbs

Preheat oven to 375°F. Salt and pepper chicken. Place each piece into the butter and then cover in the bread crumbs. Grease the bottom of each mason jar before adding the chicken. Place a piece of ham and cheese on top of each piece of chicken.

Bake for about 40 minutes. Check them after 20 minutes and if they seem to be getting too done on the top, you can cover the top with foil. Remove the foil for the last 5 minutes of cooking time.

TEX-MEX SHRIMP

2 organic tomatoes, chopped
½ cup organic onion, chopped
¼ cup organic jalapeños, chopped
¼ cup lime juice
1 pound shrimp, cooked and peeled
2 organic avocados, sliced
2 cups organic lettuce, shredded
1 cup organic tortilla chips, crumbled

Mix all the ingredients together except for the lettuce, shrimp, and chips. Place a layer of lettuce on the bottom of the mason jar. Add a generous amount of the mixed ingredients. Add a layer of shrimp and then more of the mixed ingredients. Add the chips to the top.

MINI CHICKEN POT PIES

8 mason jars, 4 ounces each

2 packages refrigerated pie crust
1/3 cup grass-fed butter
1/3 organic all-purpose flour
½ cup organic onion, chopped
1 teaspoon himalayan salt
½ teaspoon pepper
2 cups organic chicken broth, low sodium
½ cup organic milk
3 cups organic chicken, cooked and shredded
1 16-ounce can carrots, drained
1 16-ounce can peas, drained

Preheat oven to 425°F. The pie crusts should be cut into 4 quarters each. Place 1 quarter into the bottom of each jar. Melt the butter in a skillet and add the onions. Sauté them for a couple of minutes. Add the salt, pepper, and flour, mixing well. Add the broth and milk slowly and continue to stir. The mixture will thicken.

Bring the mixture to a boil and then reduce the heat to medium. Add the vegetables and heat for a few minutes. Add the chicken and allow it to get hot. Spoon the mixture into the jars, filling them almost to the top.

Place another quarter of the pie crust at the top of each jar. If possible, make a lattice pattern using thin strips of crust. This creates air vents through the dough while the jars are cooking. Bake for 15 minutes or until the dough on top is golden brown.

Ella Marie

PIZZA

6 mason jars, 4 ounces each

1 package organic pizza dough
1 16-ounce jar organic pizza sauce
2 cups grass fed mozzarella cheese
Desired toppings, such as pepperoni, bacon, vegetables (nitrate-free/organic)

Preheat oven to 375°F. Prepare pizza dough according to the directions on the package. Cook and drain any meats. Cut any vegetables you would like to use.

Place the dough on the bottom of each mason jar, about 1 inch thick. Bake for 15 to 20 minutes. The dough should be crisp and brown. Add layers of sauce, toppings and cheese. Repeat until you are almost at the top of the mason jar. Then add more dough to the top of the mason jar.

Place the jars in a baking pan with about 2 inches of water. This will prevent the bottom layer of crust from burning. Bake them for about 15 minutes. The top crust should be golden brown.

LASAGNA

12 mason jars, 8 ounces each

3 cups wide egg noodles
1 lb ricotta
1 cup Parmesan cheese
2 cups Mozzarella cheese
3 cups organic marinara sauce
2 cups grass-fed ground beef or ground sausage

Boil and prepare the noodles according to the directions on the packaging. Drain and allow them to remain in the pot on low heat. Add 2 cups of the sauce. In a bowl, mix the other ingredients except the Parmesan cheese. Add this mixture to the noodles and sauce and stir well.

Spoon the mixture into well-greased mason jars. Top them with the other cup of sauce. Sprinkle the Parmesan cheese on the top. Bake at 350°F for about 30 minutes.

Ella Marie

SHEPHERD'S PIE

6 mason jars, 6 ounces each

Topping:
3 cups organic golden potatoes, cooked and mashed
3 cups organic kale, chopped
1 leek, sliced thin
1 cup organic milk
2 tablespoons grass-fed butter
1 teaspoon himalayan salt
½ teaspoon nutmeg

Filling:
1 lb sausage, cooked and crumbled
2 tablespoons olive oil
½ cup Guinness
1 organic onion, chopped
2 organic garlic cloves, minced
1 cup organic celery, chopped
1 cup organic carrots, chopped
1 cup organic cabbage, chopped
2 tablespoons organic flour
2 teaspoons Worcestershire sauce
½ cup organic vegetable broth, low sodium
1 cup peas, drained

Topping:
1 cup white cheddar cheese, shredded

Preheat your oven to 400°F. Prepare the potatoes and put them aside to cool. In a small pot, mix the nutmeg, salt, butter, leek, kale, and milk. Stir well and allow to simmer for about 10 minutes. Add the potatoes to this mixture. Heat for a few minutes and then allow it to cool while preparing the filling.

Heat 1 tablespoon olive oil and add the sausage. Cook until brown and then drain the grease. Add the other tablespoon of olive oil and the vegetables. Sauté them for about 10 minutes until they are soft. Add the flour and stir well.

Add the Guinness and Worcestershire. Allow mixture to heat until it is thick and bubbling. Add the sausage and peas and continue to cook until everything is well-mixed and heated. Fill the jars and place them on a baking sheet. Bake at 400°F for 20 minutes. Add the cheese to the top and allow it to melt for a couple of minutes before serving.

Chapter 8
Dessert Recipes

There are plenty of delicious dessert recipes that you can make in mason jars, too. They can be a fun addition to your meal for the family. They can also be a spectacular way to show off a dessert for a special occasion.

APPLE CRUMBLE COOKIES

6 mason jars, 4 ounces each

½ cup organic flax seed
1 tablespoon organic maple syrup
3 cups organic gluten-free rolled oats
1 cup almond flour
1 teaspoon baking powder
1 teaspoon baking soda
1 teaspoon cinnamon
1 teaspoon himalayan salt
½ cup cold-pressed organic raw coconut oil
½ cup coconut sugar
2 teaspoons chia seed, ground
1 teaspoon vanilla
2 cups organic apples, diced
1 cup walnuts, optional

Mix the flax seed and maple syrup in a small bowl. Add the nuts and heat the mixture on a cookie sheet in the oven for 10 minutes at

170°F. In a large mixing bowl, add the cinnamon, salt, baking soda, oats, and baking powder. Combine well.

In another mixing bowl, combine the coconut oil with the sugar. Add the flax mix, sugar, and vanilla. Slowly add the dry wet ingredients to the mixing bowl with the dry ingredients. Stir well then add the apples.

Preheat oven to 350°F. Place 1 inch of water at the bottom of a cake pan and then add the mason jars to that pan. Spoon the mixture into the jars and cook for about 35 to 40 minutes. The cookies should be firm and pulling away from the glass when they are done.

BLUEBERRY CRISP

6 mason jars, 4 ounces each

5 cups organic blueberries, fresh
¼ cup cornstarch
½ cup coconut sugar

Filling:
½ cup coconut sugar
½ cup organic brown sugar
½ cup organic all-purpose flour
1 teaspoon himalayan salt
½ cup gluten-free rolled oats
¼ cup grass-fed butter
1 teaspoon cinnamon

In a saucepan, combine the blueberries, cornstarch, and ½ cup sugar over medium heat. The blueberries will soften and you can mash them as they cook. The mixture is done when it is thick and bubbling. Remove from the heat and let it set.

In a mixing bowl, combine the remaining ingredients. Fill the mason jars 2/3 full with the blueberries. Use the remaining 1/3 of the jar for the filling mixture. Add a bit more blueberry mix to the top if you have room.

Place the mason jars on a baking sheet and bake at 350°F for about 20 to 25 minutes. Allow them to cool for 30 minutes before eating.

IRISH WHISKEY CAKE

10 mason jars, 8 ounces each

Cake:
2 cup organic all-purpose flour
2 tablespoons baking soda
1 teaspoon himalayan salt
2 cups organic coffee, strong brewed
¼ cup Irish Whiskey
1 cup grass-fed butter, unsalted, cut in small pieces
1 teaspoon cinnamon
1 cup cocoa powder, unsweetened
2 cups coconut sugar
3 free-range eggs
1 teaspoon vanilla

Preheat oven to 325°F. Whisk the salt, baking soda, and flour well in a mixing bowl. In a saucepan, add the coffee, butter, cinnamon, cocoa powder, and whisky. Stir well over medium heat and mix until the butter is completely melted. Remove from heat and mix in the sugar. Pour the mixture into a large bowl and allow it to cool.

In another bowl, whisk the vanilla and eggs. Add it to the wet mixture. Add the flour mixture and whisk well. The mixture will be thin but it will thicken later. Don't add more flour!

Place the mason jars on a cookie sheet and fill each one ½ full with the batter. Bake for 45 to 55 minutes depending on oven variations.

RED VELVET CUPCAKES

12 mason jars, 4 ounces each

Cupcakes:
1 cup cake flour
2 tablespoons cocoa powder, unsweetened
1 teaspoon himalayan salt
2/3 cups coconut oil
1 cup coconut sugar
1 free-range egg
1 teaspoon vanilla
4 drops red food coloring (beet derived)
½ cup organic buttermilk
1 teaspoon baking soda
1 teaspoon white vinegar

Cream Cheese Icing:
8 ounces organic cream cheese, softened
3 tablespoons grass-fed butter, softened
3 cups powdered sugar, sifted
2 teaspoons vanilla

Preheat oven to 350°F. Sift the cake flour, salt, and cocoa powder in a mixing bowl. Add the egg and oil and mix well. Add the vanilla and food coloring. Add the buttermilk but don't over mix. Add the baking soda and then the vinegar, mixing after each.

Divide the batter into the 12 mason jars. Don't fill them more than 2/3 full. Bake for 20 to 24 minutes. While they are baking make your cream cheese icing. Mix the butter and cream cheese well. Add the powdered sugar a little at a time and mix well. Add the vanilla.

After the cupcakes are done, use a knife to slice down the middle of each one. Pour your icing into the opening so the icing will reach the bottom of the mason jar. You will get some of the delicious icing with each bite of these amazing red velvet cupcakes.

NO-BAKE LEMON CHEESECAKE

12 mason jars, 8 ounces each

Lemon Layer:
7 free-range eggs, yolks only
2 free-range eggs, whole
1 ¼ cup coconut sugar
½ cup lemon juice, fresh
¼ cup lemon zest
A pinch of himalayan salt
4 tablespoons grass-fed butter
3 teaspoons organic heavy cream

Whisk all the eggs well and place them into a saucepan. Add the sugar, lemon juice, zest, butter, and salt. Whisk well while it is heating. It will take about 10 minutes to thicken. Stir often to prevent it from burning on the bottom. Pour the mixture through a sieve and then add the cream. Whisk well. Cover and refrigerate for at least 2 hours.

Cheesecake Layer:
1 cup organic heavy cream
½ cup coconut sugar
32 ounces organic cream cheese, softened

Mix cream and sugar together on high until stiff peaks are created. Reduce the mixer to low speed and add the cream cheese. Continue to mix until it is smooth.

Graham Cracker Layer:
15 graham crackers
6 tablespoons grass-fed butter, melted

Blend the graham crackers so they are finely crushed. Mix well with the melted butter.

Press the graham cracker mixture into the bottom of each mason jar. Add the cheesecake mixture. Add the lemon layer. Allow the dessert to chill for a couple of hours before serving. Top with whipped cream if desired.

Ella Marie

COCONUT CREAM AND TROPICAL RUM TRIFLE

6 mason jars, 4 ounces each

Coconut Cream:
1 cup coconut sugar
¼ cup cornstarch
1 cup organic milk
14 ounces coconut milk, unsweetened
4 free-range eggs, yolks only

Trifle:
4 cups organic mango, pineapple, and strawberries, chopped and well mixed
¼ cup coconut sugar
¼ cup rum
3 cups coconut cream
1 pound cake, cut into pieces
½ cup coconut, shredded
1 cup macadamia nuts, chopped

Whisk both types of milk, eggs, cornstarch, and sugar in a saucepan over medium heat. Cook for about 5 minutes while stirring often to prevent lumps. Pour the mixture through a strainer and refrigerate for at least 2 hours.

Mix the fruit with the sugar and rum. Allow it to sit for 30 minutes. Strain but keep the liquid. Pour the liquid over the cake chunks. Add pieces of the cake to the mason jars. Add fruit and then a layer of the coconut cream. Chill for at least 2 hours before serving.

FLOUR-LESS CHOCOLATE CAKE

12 mason jars, 8 ounces each

7 ounces bittersweet baking chocolate
½ stick grass-fed butter, unsalted
1 cup coconut sugar
4 free-range eggs, separated
¼ cup powdered sugar

Preheat oven to 350°F. Lightly grease the jars on the sides and the bottom. Using a double boiler, melt the chocolate. When it is almost melted add the butter. Continue to heat until the mixture is smooth. Remove from heat and allow it to cool.

In a mixing bowl beat the egg whites until stiff peaks form. In another bowl, add the egg yolks and sugar, mix until they are creamy and thick. Slowly add the melted chocolate mixture to the egg yolk mixture. Fold the egg whites into the mixture.

Place the jars on a baking sheet and fill them up with the cake batter. Don't fill more than 1/3 full. Bake for 25 to 30 minutes. They are done when the top of the cake starts to crack. Remove from the oven and allow the jars to fully cool. Dust the tops with the powdered sugar.

Ella Marie

CHERRY CRISP

4 mason jars, 8 ounces each

3 cups cherry pie filling
½ cup organic all-purpose flour
½ cup gluten-free rolled oats
1/3 cup brown sugar, packed
¼ cup grass-fed butter, melted

Preheat oven to 350°F. Place the pie filling into the bottom of the mason jars. In a large bowl, mix the other ingredients well. Spoon the mixture on top of the cherries in the mason jars. Bake for 20 to 25 minutes. Serve warm with whipped cream or ice cream if desired.

MINI BLACKBERRY PIES

6 mason jars, 4 ounces each

4 cups organic blackberries, frozen or fresh
1 cup coconut sugar
1 teaspoon lemon zest
¼ teaspoon cinnamon
2 tablespoons organic flour
2 tablespoons grass-fed butter
1 free-range egg, beaten
1 package pie dough

Mix the blueberries, sugar, cinnamon, flour, and lemon zest. If you use frozen blueberries, thaw them before you start. Fill the mason jars with the mixture. The mixture will sink as it bakes, so don't worry if the mason jars look too full.

Add ¼ tablespoon of butter to each jar. Cut the dough into ¼" strips. Make a lattice top with 4 strips one way, 3 strips the other way. Brush the lattice with the beaten egg and place on top of the blackberry mixture

Bake for 20 minutes at 375 °. Allow to cool slightly and then serve while still warm. Add whipped cream or ice cream if desired.

Ella Marie

CHOCOLATE STRAWBERRY PARFAIT

This recipe is per mason jar

1 cup organic plain yogurt
2/3 cup gluten-free granola
6 organic strawberries, sliced
2 ounce chocolate bar, broken into pieces

Add half of the yogurt to the bottom of the mason jar. Add half of the granola. Add three strawberries and half of the chocolate. Repeat for a second layer.

Conclusion

Mason jar breakfasts, lunches, and desserts are a fun and classy way to bring some excitement back into your eating. Now that you know what it takes and you have some amazing recipes to try, what are you waiting for? Once you try it out, you won't go back to your normal methods of preparing food again.

There are so many benefits to making meals in mason jars:

- Less food is wasted.
- Portion control is easier and visual.
- The jars allow you to see what's inside your meal.
- The colors and layers are visually appealing.
- Mason jars keep the refrigerator cleaner and more organized.
- Glass jars are easier to clean than plastic containers and are less damaging to the environment

Trial and error are a part of any cooking adventures. With that in mind, don't be shy about giving mason jar food options a try. You will love the way they turn out. Search for recipes that have ingredients that you and your family will really enjoy.

You don't have to invest a ton of money in the mason jars or the foods you need to eat healthier. It is going to cost you far less to make mason jar salads to take for lunch than to go to a fast food place every day. It is also going to be better for your overall health.

You can get your entire family looking forward to meals once again with mason jars. They are going to enjoy the change. During the warmer season, bypass the paper plates! Serve dinner in mason jars on the back porch. You can also eat dinner in the house but have a relaxing dessert in the family room.

Mason jar meals can also be a terrific way to help out others. Maybe you know someone who had surgery or just had a baby. Taking them dinner is a common practice, but taking them dinner and dessert in mason jars is going to be remembered!

They will really appreciate the special effort you have made, too. Of course you don't have to tell them how quick and easy they were to put together. That can be your secret!

You can also dress them up for gifts for special occasions or the holidays. People love to get mason jars filled with cocoa mix or the ingredients to make cookies from scratch. You can add colorful bows or decorate the jars. It can be fun to allow your creative side to flow as you make them.

Giving them as gifts may also inspire others to try out mason jar meals. Once they eat what you've given them, they can clean and reuse the jars. Perhaps that is all the motivation they need to try one of the recipes. Once they do, they will be hooked and it will become a common venture in their kitchen as well.

There really are limitless possibilities when it comes to foods in mason jars. This book offers you only a sample of them so you can get started on the right foot. Be creative and come up with your own ideas. Mason jar preparation is here to stay. It is only going to continue to evolve and that is something you will want to be a part of.

You'll also know with confidence that your family will love some of these recipes, and they will ask for them again and again! There will be no more groaning that they are tired of eating the same foods you just made last week. It's a winning situation for everyone.

Did you Like "Mason Jar Meals"?

Before you go, I'd like to say thank you so much for purchasing my book.

I know you could have picked from dozens of books on this subject, but you took a chance with mine, and I'm truly grateful for that.

So, once again, a big thanks for downloading this book and reading all the way to the end—I truly appreciate it.

Now I'd like to ask for a small favor if you don't mind:

Would you be so kind as to take a minute of your time and leave a review for this book on Amazon?

This feedback will help me continue to write the kind of books that help you get results. And if you loved it, then please feel free to let me know! :)

More Books By Ella Marie:

Baking Soda Cure: Discover the Amazing Power and Health Benefits of Baking Soda, its History and Uses For Cooking, Cleaning, and Curing Ailments

Essential Oils For Beginners: The Little Known Secrets to Essential Oils and Aromatherapy for Weight Loss, Beauty and Healing

Yoga For Beginners: The Ultimate Beginner Yoga Guide to Lose Weight, Relieve Stress and Tone Your Body With Yoga

Leptin Resistance: The Ultimate Leptin Resistance Diet Guide For Weight Loss Including Delicious Recipes And How to Overcome Leptin Resistance Naturally

DASH Diet For Weight Loss: The Ultimate Beginner Dash Diet Guide For Weight Loss, Lower Blood Pressure, and Better Health Including Delicious Dash Diet Recipes

Mindfulness For Beginners: 25 Easy Mindfulness Exercises To Help You Live In The Present Moment, Conquer Anxiety And Stress, And Have A Fulfilling Life with Mindfulness Meditation

Vegan Slow Cooker: The Ultimate Vegan Slow Cooker Cookbook Including 39 Easy & Delicious Vegan Slow Cooker Recipes For Breakfast, Lunch & Dinner!

Herbal Antibiotics: 56 Little Known Natural and Holistic Remedies To Help Cure And Prevent Bacterial Illnesses

Printed in Great Britain
by Amazon.co.uk, Ltd.,
Marston Gate.